Facing Life's Challenges

FACING PEER PRESSURE

BY GOLRIZ GOLKAR

BLUE OWL BOOKS

TIPS FOR CAREGIVERS

Social and emotional learning (SEL) helps children manage emotions, create and achieve goals, maintain relationships, learn how to feel empathy, and make good decisions. The SEL approach will help children establish positive habits in communication, cooperation, and decision-making. By incorporating SEL in early reading, children will be better equipped to build confidence and foster positive peer networks.

BEFORE READING

Talk to the reader about peer pressure. Explain how peer pressure can make a person feel uncomfortable and unsure of how to behave.

Discuss: Have you ever experienced peer pressure? How did it make you feel? Have you ever seen someone else experience it? How did you react?

AFTER READING

Talk to the reader about responding to peer pressure. Discuss things to say when feeling pressured and when witnessing peer pressure.

Discuss: How can you respond when you feel pressured by your peers? What can you do or say when you see someone experiencing peer pressure?

SEL GOAL

Students who experience peer pressure may feel uneasy. Help readers think of ways to speak up confidently when pressured. Help them think about how they can avoid pressuring others. How can they engage in positive behaviors that promote friendship, confidence, and safety?

TABLE OF CONTENTS

CHAPTER 1
What Is Peer Pressure? 4

CHAPTER 2
What You Can Do 8

CHAPTER 3
Helping Others 16

GOALS AND TOOLS
Grow with Goals 22
Try This! 22
Glossary 23
To Learn More 23
Index 24

CHAPTER 1

WHAT IS PEER PRESSURE?

Eddie's friends want to steal candy from the teacher's desk. They ask Eddie to join them. Eddie wants to fit in. But he knows stealing is wrong. Eddie is facing **peer pressure**.

Peers can **influence** the way you think or act. An example of this could be friends **gossiping** and expecting you to join. Another example could be your teammates pressuring you to skip practice.

CHAPTER 1   5

Kira wants to play a joke on someone. Ana feels **anxious**. She isn't sure it's a good idea. She is afraid she'll upset Kira if she doesn't go along with it.

Experiencing peer pressure can make you feel confused or sad. You may think your peers will tease you or leave you out if you don't join.

ASK FOR HELP

Peer pressure can lead to unsafe or unhealthy choices. You could get in trouble at school or with the law. If you ever feel scared, ask a trusted adult for help.

CHAPTER 1

CHAPTER 2
WHAT YOU CAN DO

It is important to speak up when you feel pressured. You need to be **confident** so you can make good decisions. Remember, real friends will respect your choices.

During a test, Laura passes Rosie a note. It has answers to questions on the test. This is **direct peer pressure**. Rosie is forced to make a quick decision. She feels uncomfortable. She tells Laura she doesn't want to cheat.

If direct peer pressure happens to you, say you don't like being pressured. If you are uncomfortable, you can say your parents don't allow it. You can say "no thanks" or "I'm busy." You can walk away.

CHAPTER 2

You may feel pressured to follow your peers, even if they don't ask you to. This is **indirect peer pressure**. One example is feeling the need to dress like your peers to fit in. Or you may feel pressured to like the same music. If your peers tease someone, you may feel you need to join them.

You can **avoid** peers who make you feel uncomfortable. Reed didn't like how his friends made fun of others. Now, he spends time with friends who stand up to peer pressure. They do activities everyone enjoys.

DEALING WITH FEELINGS

When you feel pressured, write down your feelings. Talk about them with a friend or trusted adult. That person can help you practice how to answer next time.

CHAPTER 2

CHAPTER 3

HELPING OTHERS

Help others stand up to peer pressure. Jan's classmates tell her to cut in line, but she doesn't want to. Leah stands next to Jan. She tells Jan she **supports** her.

Others can join you in speaking up. Jenny thinks Marcus isn't good at soccer. She tells her friends not to pass him the ball. They disagree. Together, they make sure everyone is included.

If you see someone standing up to peer pressure, join them. Say "I agree" or "let's go." Walk away together.

Speaking up together **encourages** everyone to be confident. This helps everyone make good decisions.

MAKING FRIENDS

Speaking up for others can end peer pressure. It can also create **empathy** and build friendships.

Practice good **habits** as a group. Study for tests together or practice for team sports. You can **volunteer** for a cause that's important to you. Together, you can end peer pressure by practicing safe and healthy habits.

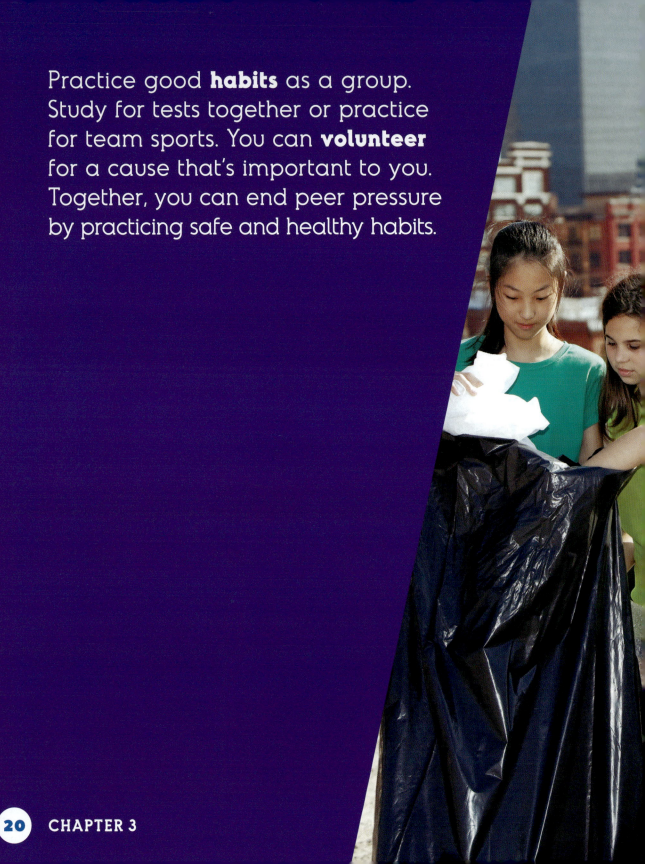

GOALS AND TOOLS

GROW WITH GOALS

Seeing or experiencing peer pressure can make you feel confused or upset. Try following these goals to help you handle these experiences.

Goal: Make a list of examples of peer pressure you have experienced or seen.

Goal: Think about how peer pressure makes you feel. Have you ever pressured anyone? Why do you think you did this? Ask your friends if they have experienced it. How did it make them feel?

Goal: With a friend, discuss ways to respond to peer pressure. Think of things you could say when pressured. Discuss some good habits you can follow together to stand up to peer pressure and stop pressuring others.

TRY THIS!

Have you ever experienced or seen peer pressure that made people feel unsafe? With a friend, practice how you might handle these situations.

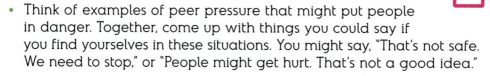

- Think of examples of peer pressure that might put people in danger. Together, come up with things you could say if you find yourselves in these situations. You might say, "That's not safe. We need to stop," or "People might get hurt. That's not a good idea."

- Think of ways to ask trusted adults for help. You might say, "Those kids are pressuring us to do things we don't want to do. We are afraid people will get hurt or in trouble."

- Ask an adult to help you practice how to respond to peer pressure.

GLOSSARY

anxious
Worried or very eager to do something.

avoid
To stay away from something or to try to prevent something from happening.

confident
Self-assured and having a strong belief in your own abilities.

direct peer pressure
Being asked to do something you wouldn't normally do or being placed in a situation in which you have to make a quick decision.

empathy
The ability to understand and be sensitive to the thoughts and feelings of others.

encourages
Gives someone confidence, usually by using praise and support.

gossiping
Spreading rumors or saying things about a person that may not be true.

habits
Activities and behaviors that you do regularly, often without thinking about them.

indirect peer pressure
Seeing or hearing peers behave a certain way and feeling pressured to follow them.

influence
To have an effect on someone or something.

peer pressure
A feeling that you must do what other peers, or people of your age and social group, are doing in order for them to like you.

supports
Gives help, comfort, or encouragement to someone or something.

volunteer
To do a job without pay.

TO LEARN MORE

Finding more information is as easy as 1, 2, 3.

1. Go to www.factsurfer.com
2. Enter "**facingpeerpressure**" into the search box.
3. Choose your book to see a list of websites.

INDEX

activities 14

adult 6, 14

anxious 6

cheat 9

choices 6, 8

confident 8, 19

confused 6

decisions 8, 9, 19

direct peer pressure 9, 10

empathy 19

feelings 14

friends 4, 5, 8, 14, 17, 19

gossiping 5

habits 20

included 17

indirect peer pressure 13

peers 5, 6, 13, 14

pressuring 5, 8, 10, 13, 14

sad 6

speak up 8, 17, 19

steal 4

talk 14

tease 6, 13

uncomfortable 9, 10, 14

upset 6

write 14

Blue Owl Books are published by Jump!, 5357 Penn Avenue South, Minneapolis, MN 55419, www.jumplibrary.com

Copyright © 2023 Jump! International copyright reserved in all countries. No part of this book may be reproduced in any form without written permission from the publisher.

Library of Congress Cataloging-in-Publication Data
Names: Golkar, Golriz, author.
Title: Facing peer pressure / by Golriz Golkar.
Description: Minneapolis, MN: Jump!, Inc., [2023] | Series: Facing life's challenges | Includes index. | Audience: Ages 7–10
Identifiers: LCCN 2021056326 (print)
LCCN 2021056327 (ebook)
ISBN 9781636908137 (hardcover)
ISBN 9781636908144 (paperback)
ISBN 9781636908151 (ebook)
Subjects: LCSH: Peer pressure–Juvenile literature. | Peer pressure in children–Juvenile literature. | Peer pressure in adolescence–Juvenile literature.
Classification: LCC HQ784.P43 G66 2023 (print)
LCC HQ784.P43 (ebook) | DDC 155.4/192–dc23/eng/20211130
LC record available at https://lccn.loc.gov/2021056326
LC ebook record available at https://lccn.loc.gov/2021056327

Editor: Eliza Leahy
Designer: Molly Ballanger

Photo Credits: Zoja Hussainova/Shutterstock, cover (left); kostudio/Shutterstock, cover (right); Shutterstock, 1; bagussatria/Shutterstock, 3; Alina555/iStock, 4 (left); Asier Romero/Shutterstock, 4 (right); Jupiterimages/Getty, 5; Just dance/Shutterstock, 6–7; MoMo Productions/Getty, 8; Comstock Images/Getty, 9; A Sharma/Shutterstock, 10–11; supersizer/iStock, 12–13; PeopleImages/iStock, 14–15; feeling lucky/Shutterstock, 16; FatCamera/iStock, 17; SDI Productions/Getty, 18–19; JBryson/iStock, 20–21.

Printed in the United States of America at Corporate Graphics in North Mankato, Minnesota.

GOALS AND TOOLS